Mountain of Crime

A Murder Mystery Comedy by
Francis RTM Boyle & James Mainard O'Connell

Uproar Theatrics

LICENSING & PRODUCTION INQUIRIES
Uproar Theatrics, LLC.
hello@uproartheatrics.com I www.UproarTheatrics.com

Mountain of Crime, A Murder Mystery Comedy
copyright © 2024 by James Mainard O'Connell & Francis RTM Boyle

Mountain of Crime, A Murder Mystery Comedy is published by
Uproar Theatrics, LLC, 500 8th Ave FRNT 3, #1714 New York, NY 10018

ISBN: 978-1-968051-11-2

First Printing, May 2025

Characters:

The Don:	Male, 30-50. Head of the National Crime Syndicate.
Vanessa:	Female, 30-50. The Don's wife.
Butch:	Male, 20s-40s. The Don's goon.
Lucky:	Male, 30-50. Head of the Kentucky Crime Syndicate.
Red:	Female, 30-50. Head of the Boston Crime Syndicate.
Hungry:	Male, 30-50. Head of the New York Crime Syndicate.
Honey:	Female, 20s-40. Butch's girlfriend.
Marlowe:	Male, 30-50. Twin brother of The Don. May be played by the same actor as The Don or separate actors.

Setting:
Wherever the show is performing. Any references to the physical location may be altered to fit the performance location.

Staging and Intermission Note:
This play was written for Environmental Theatre in which the performers and audience share the same space; no stage is required. Additionally, it is written with the possibility of dinner theatre in mind, so there are three optional breaks in the action to serve food.

Recommended use of optional dinner scene breaks:
Before the Show: Drinks
After Scene 1: Appetizers and/or salad
After Scene 2: Main course
After Scene 3: Dessert

Play Length:
Mountain of Crime can run anywhere from 50-120 minutes or longer. The reason for this range is because of the variability in the length of the improvisational moments as well as flexibility regarding the scene breaks. A performance of the play with no breaks and limited audience interaction would yield a performance approximately 50-60 minutes, while a performance with a great deal of audience interaction and lengthy food service breaks could yield up to or beyond an additional 60 minutes.

Choosing a Killer:
This play includes six different possible endings. Feel free to choose whichever ending best suits the production's needs. If you have a long run, doing a different ending each performance is a lot of fun and rewards multiple viewings. You have the option of deciding the killer prior to the performance or waiting until after scene 3 when you see the audience's guesses.

Prologue

(Prior to the show, the audience should be sectioned into three groups which represent LUCKY's gang, RED's gang, and HUNGRY's gang. The show begins improvisationally, with the three gang leaders entering and each mingling and speaking with their gang.)

LUCKY, RED, and HUNGRY
(What each of these characters says to their gang of audience members is improvised, but it should include the following.)

- Introduce yourself to the gang. In the context of the play, they would already know who you are, so be creative.
- Welcome the gang and thank them for coming.
- Learn the names of some of the people, or, if you prefer, you can give them names of your choosing.
- Select one member of the gang to be your deputy. Make it clear you will call on them for help later. If your gang consists of multiple sections, such as separate tables, you may assign one deputy per section.
- Get them on your side and make it clear that they shouldn't trust the other gangs.
- Tell them to stay calm and let you do the talking throughout the evening unless you call on them to do something.

Scene 1

(MARLOWE enters with an unlit cigar. He speaks to the whole audience as LUCKY, RED, and HUNGRY busy themselves quietly.)

MARLOWE

It was a dark and stormy night in/at *[wherever the show happens to be]*: a sort of place that looks beautiful to the untrained eye, but hides its secrets under a cloak of mystery and misbegotten circumstance. A place where any night or day can be one to haunt your memory for years to come. But this particular night...this night I will never forget. The kind of night when you just know someone's going to end up in the meat-wagon. The National Crime Syndicate, the governing body of all the major crime organizations in the country, called a meeting. The sort of meeting that would make any police officer pee his pants and scream like a little girl at the thought of it. A meeting of the three biggest crime organizations in the country – the Boston Syndicate, the New York Syndicate, and the Kentucky Syndicate. Over there is the head of the Kentucky Syndicate. People call him Lucky because of his lucky flask that he carries with him at all times. Over there is the boss of Boston, Maureen Kathryn Sinead O'Callaghan-McGee. People call her Red because she's Irish. And because of her red-hot temper. And because she likes the color red. Finally, we have the head of the New York Syndicate, "Hungry" Luciano. Nobody knows his real name. He goes by "Hungry" for obvious reasons – he always wants food. One catch though – he's a militant vegetarian. How do I know all this? I'm the twin brother of the man in charge. They call me Marlowe. I used to be a detective for the *[town neighboring the performance location]* police department. Then I lost my eye in a bar fight a few years back- so now I'm a private eye. Yeah, I got regrets. But back to the matter at hand. There's gonna be a murder here tonight. The sort of murder that'll make even the most

MARLOWE (CONT)

seasoned detective scratch his head and say, "I don't know who did it." But, that's not what I came here to tell you. I'm gonna let this story play out in front of you so you can draw your own conclusions. I'll be back, so you'd better behave yourselves and play along.

(He exits.)

LUCKY

Hey y'all, Red, Hungry – I wanna talk at you. *(He drinks from his flask.)*

RED

Whatcha gonna say if I decide not to listen, boy-oh? I've got me own stuff to worry about.

HUNGRY

Yeah. I've got a nice, tasty salad over here.

LUCKY

Look, I know you know that we need to talk some business before the Don shows up.

RED

What's to talk about? You got some trouble with your business you need our help for?

LUCKY

I just want to figure out what we're all doing here.

HUNGRY

Power-

RED

Aye, he wants more of it. Even though he's got everything.

LUCKY

Shucks, he could be rounding us all up to kill us, you think of that?

HUNGRY

That's why I brought some of my best people with me. *(He indicates to his portion of the audience.)* More of us than him. Standard procedure. Looks like you did the same.

RED

What's the matter Lucky? Worried your flask won't protect you?

LUCKY

Listen Red, this flask took a bullet for me three years back, and I'm gonna keep it until the day I die. Maybe y'all would do good to have some luck on you.

RED

Ah, but I do. Her name is Samantha, she's a .45, and she'll go right through your lucky flask.

HUNGRY

We're not supposed to be carrying. That was explicit. Man, I love spinach.

LUCKY

Yeah, Red. You pull that thing on me, and you're gonna get it from the Don himself.

RED

You watch him try to take me weapon off me. We'll see who's running the show once Samantha puts one through him. I'd run things far better than him.

HUNGRY

Just because nepotism got him this far doesn't mean that he doesn't run a tight ship. Although he'd do a lot better if he'd stop working with the beef industry. They're more corrupt than any of us.

RED

You take no risks, you gain nothing. That man runs things just like his father, and you know times have changed.

LUCKY

Shut your yap, I think he's coming.

RED

Oh, it's just Butch.

> (BUTCH *enters, carrying a brick. He speaks to the whole room.*)

BUTCH

Everybody look up here. Okay. *(He takes out a wadded-up piece of paper from his pocket and reads it with some difficulty.)* "I have sent Butch ahead of me to ensure that you are each present. Vanessa and I will arrive shortly. I trust that you are unarmed and Butch will not need to disarm you. Yours, The Don." Okay. Lucky.

LUCKY

Yeah.

BUTCH

Okay. Red.

RED

Of course I'm here you dumb lout.

BUTCH

Okay. Hungry.

HUNGRY

Here.

BUTCH

Okay. *(Walks to the door from which he entered.)* They're all here boss. I haven't had to use my brick yet. You wanna come in now? Okay. *(Turns back to address the room.)* Everyone stand now. *(Hopefully everyone in the audience will stand. If not, he can repeat it more emphatically.)* Okay. Here comes The Don. If you try to shoot him, I will beat you with my brick.

> *(Enter DON, VANESSA, and HONEY. HONEY goes straight to BUTCH and kisses him on the cheek.)*

HONEY

Great speech, sweetie. You're so eloquent.

BUTCH

Thank you.

HONEY

You get a reward later.

DON

(Addressing everyone, perhaps with a microphone.) Thank you Butch, for that rousing introduction. You may all sit. Except for you: Lucky, Red, and Hungry. As you know, I only invited you three to this gathering. Of course, I was smart enough to assume that you would not come alone, so I had my people set enough places for your various entourages. Still, your unwillingness to come alone is a violation of my trust, which I do not take lightly. My lovely

DON (CONT)

wife Vanessa here shared her opinion on the subject just a moment ago. Dear, would you mind sharing how you would have dealt with this situation?

VANESSA

I would have gassed the building, torched it, and left, but my husband believes in charity.

DON

I believe in trust. And there's no trust in death. If you again violate my trust tonight, you won't know what fell on you. Do I make that clear, Lucky?

LUCKY

Yeah.

DON

Red?

RED

Sure.

DON

Hungry?

HUNGRY

Absolutely.

DON

Good. Before I continue, I must know who it is who shares my room. Why don't you introduce me to your most important people. Lucky? *(LUCKY introduces his appointed officers from among his gang.)* Welcome. Red? *(RED introduces her appointed officers.)* Nice to see you. Hungry? *(HUNGRY introduces his appointed officers.)* Excellent. Although none of you were invited, you are here,

DON (CONT)

and I must be gracious. Two rules. One. When I am in the building, you answer to me, not Lucky, Red, or Hungry. If you don't answer to me, you will have to answer to Butch and his brick.

BUTCH

I love my brick. My brick loves your face.

DON

Thank you, Butch. Two. When I am in the building, nobody carries a gun but Vanessa, Butch and I. Anybody carrying will answer to Butch and his brick.

BUTCH

She loves kneecaps too.

DON

Thank you, Butch.

BUTCH

Oh, and the mastoid process.

DON

Now I'm sure you're wondering why I've called you here.

LUCKY

If you plan to kill us it ain't happenin'.

DON

Butch, go stand by Lucky.

BUTCH

Okay.

(BUTCH moves next to LUCKY.)

DON

If I was planning to kill you, I'd have done it by now, and it wouldn't be here. I'm here to announce my retirement.

RED

Holy Saint Pat, preserve and defend us from evil and red cabbage.

LUCKY

Well, I'll be.

HUNGRY

Why aren't there any croutons in my salad?

DON

Hungry. Pay attention please.

HUNGRY

Of course.

(He puts down his fork.)

DON

I know that I am young. I climbed to the top of this mountain of crime faster than most. I also know that I have only held this position for five years, but that is long enough. I have the money that I need, and I'm tired of the stress. I plan to lead for another six months. After which, one of you will succeed me. I have called you here tonight to lay plans for a smooth transition of power. But before we get moving on that, my wife and I are going to step outside for a smoke. I leave Butch in charge of keeping things in order. Do not make Butch use his brick. Vanessa.

(DON and VANESSA exit.)

HONEY
Hungry, I wish you all the luck in the world.

HUNGRY
Luck won't have nothing to do with it, baby. But don't go anywhere. I'm gonna go find a bathroom.

(Exit HUNGRY.)

RED
Butch, dear heart, I've got something to show you.

BUTCH
Okay. Wow, it's tense in here.

(Exit BUTCH and RED.)

LUCKY
Honey, what are you doing going 'round with that brick loving idiot? Boy did you draw the short straw on that one or what?

HONEY
Lucky darling, a girl may run to any man after she's abandoned by perfection. You never said goodbye.

LUCKY
Just one minute, Honey Buhns. You walked out on me.

HONEY
Let us not argue, my love. You were mad then, it is true. You broke my heart and you know it.

LUCKY
You threw your makeup case through my windshield. Darlin' you've got issues and I worry about you.

HONEY

Lucky, how could you be so cruel after what I've been
through?

No one understands, no one can understand, the vast deep
ocean that is this poor, simple, lonely girl's heart. No one, no
one except you- all along.

Oh, why did you leave me Lucky? I love you.

Don't try to speak, I know you care. The truth is I don't even
like Butch, or his brick. I knew you'd be here, and that's
what I'm after.

LUCKY

I'm here, sugar, I'm here.

HONEY

I just don't know whatever I would do if I lost you again.

LUCKY

You don't need to, sugar, you don't need to.

HONEY

I'm afraid of that man and his brick. I can't leave him until
we're done here.

LUCKY

Sure, sugar. Until then, it's "Mum's the word."

HONEY

Someone's coming.

LUCKY

Red and Hungry.

> (*Enter* RED *and* HUNGRY. RED *turns her*
> *attention to* LUCKY *as* HUNGRY *and* HONEY
> *speak in the background. At some point in the*
> *next page or so,* BUTCH *re-enters, generally*

11

looking menacing but apparently oblivious to
HONEY's *interactions with the other*
characters. Sometime before his next line, he
exits to wherever DON *exited.*)

RED

What are you looking so satisfied about, boy-oh? I bet you think the Don's going to make you his successor, well not if I have anything to say about it. What have you got to say for yourself, hey Lucky?

Shut up when I'm berating you. I bet you think the sun shines right out of your arse, don't you? Oh, what's a matter? Someone not give you enough love when you were a wee little baby, and now, dejected, you've turned to a life of crime- is that it? Is it?

Now don't you dare be talkin' back to me, buck-oh, or Samantha will introduce you to a whole universe of pain. Now what you be thinking about that my lanky friend?

LUCKY

Hi Red.

RED

Now don't you be taking liberties with my name dear heart- I'll make you bleed or my name isn't Maureen Kathryn Sinead O'Callaghan-McGee.

LUCKY

I meant no offense.

RED

Oh, I could just eat you up you big softy lummox. You've got the gift of the Blarney, you silver tongued she-tamer. How 'bout a kiss?

LUCKY

No thanks.

12

RED
Oh well. Piss off then. Oi, Vanessa!

(Enter Vanessa. Focus shifts to HONEY and HUNGRY.)

HONEY
Hungry, how could you be so cruel after what I've been through?
No one understands, no one can understand, the vast deep ocean that is this poor, simple, lonely girl's heart. No one, no one except you- all along.
Oh, why did you leave me Hungry? I love you.
Don't try to speak, I know you care. The truth is I don't even like Butch, or his brick. I knew you'd be here, and that's what I'm after.

HUNGRY
Baby, you know I need you. You're the only woman on the Earth who loves flan covered grape-leaf based mi krop as much as I do. Come back with me and it will be like old times, I promise. You won't have to do anything you don't want to.

HONEY
I'm afraid of that man and his brick. I can't leave him until we're done here.

HUNGRY
Don't you worry- I've got everything taken care of.

HONEY
You have no idea how much I love you.

(VANESSA approaches the conversation.)

VANESSA

Hungry.

HUNGRY

Yes?

VANESSA

A word?

(HONEY takes RED aside.)

HUNGRY

Vegetable.

VANESSA

What? No, dammit, a word with you. The Don has a
message for all the family heads.

HUNGRY

You don't look like Butch. Shouldn't he be delivering this
message? Or is he off somewhere "polishing his brick?"

VANESSA

Butch is only good at two things- speaking in monosyllables
or delivering brick-based learning experiences. This message
requires a bit more panache.

HUNGRY

Go on.

VANESSA

The Don knows that announcing his retirement came as a
shock to everyone- and he's ordering all of you to make a
formal statement of why you should be the boss.

HUNGRY

When?

VANESSA

Soon enough. Everyone will be there so it better be good.

HUNGRY

Thanks, Vanessa. Tell me- will you miss all this?

VANESSA

All what?

HUNGRY

This- The power. You're the woman behind the man. You
have his ear, his automatic respect and you can control
access to him. All that goes away when he's retired. That is a
lot of power to lose.

VANESSA

Yes, it is. And that's a remarkably premeditated comment.
What do you want?

HUNGRY

A shame you don't have much time to use your influence.
But you have just enough time to use it again.

VANESSA

For you?

HUNGRY

Help your husband realize that I am the best man for his job.

VANESSA

That's what Red and Lucky just said. Why should I help
you?

HUNGRY

I know how it feels to be powerless in a world that needs
your strength.

VANESSA

Cut the philosophy. What are you offering me?

HUNGRY

Name your price.

VANESSA

You should be careful, Mr. Luciano. Those three little words can be more costly than you realize. There's no telling what I might say back. We'll talk later.

(VANESSA *and* HUNGRY *part ways, and focus shifts to* HONEY *and* RED.)

HONEY

Red, how could you be so cruel after what I've been through? No one understands, no one can understand, the vast deep ocean that is this poor, simple, lonely girl's heart. No one, no one except you- all along.
Oh, why did you leave me Red? I love you.
Don't try to speak, I know you care. The truth is I don't even like Butch, or his brick. I knew you'd be here, and that's what I'm after.

RED

Oh, take heart, my love. You need not be a-fearing your old Red, eh? We've had a tussle and that's it. Brace up, and you let "Reddy" take care of it.

HONEY

I'm afraid of that man and his brick. Oh Lord, here he comes now.

(BUTCH *re-enters.*)

BUTCH

You can come in, boss, they're all here.

HONEY

Oh schnuck-ems!

BUTCH

Hi Honey. I like your face.

(Enter DON.)

DON

Alright. Now everyone gather 'round. This is how we will do this. Lucky, Red, Hungry- each of you will tell me the reason that you deserve my job. If anyone doesn't want my job, they can leave now. Anyone? Good. Red.

RED

Yes sir?

DON

You're up.

RED

But I'm second.

DON

I'm a man of enigmas. Why do you want my job?

RED

The money and the power, silly.

DON

You're honest, I'll give you that. But let's not forget that this thing of ours is secret and we have to keep it that way. So much of keeping a secret is a cool head, and you do not have the kind of temperament that is conducive to keeping a low profile.

RED

How do you mean? I'm naught but a wee Boston housewife. I am urbane and level-headed and I'll castrate the man who says otherwise.

LUCKY

Real level-headed.

DON

Let's not get personal here. We don't want to have another "Providence"-like episode, do we Red?

RED

How dare you?

HUNGRY

Wait a minute- what happened in Providence, Red?

RED

Nothing.

LUCKY

Doesn't sound that way to me. What happened Boss?

DON

Do you want to tell them, Red?

RED

One of the Providence bosses disliked my Chowder. I taught them how to make it.

DON

She took half of the Providence thugs and made *them* into her next batch of Chowder.

RED

See- nothing.

DON

Which she then fed to the bosses. It cost a lot of money to keep the Providence hounds away. All for your temper, Red.

LUCKY

That proves it boss, she can't have your job.

DON

Can't she Lucky? Don't you think there are other wastes of resources than anger?

LUCKY

Boss, you said you wouldn't tell a soul.

RED

No no, let's hear it.

DON

Now you all know this redneck's crew. And you know you can't get any respect in the Kentucky Crime families unless you're a poor country boy. But this man isn't poor, and his name is not "Lucky." His real name is Marbury Clinton the Third- son of a wealthy bluegrass dealer.
But to get his "street cred"- he posed as a hick in a trailer park. Someone got wise and suddenly the whole trailer park is blackmailing him. Lucky, oh I mean Marbury gave me a call and the best part of that park is now under a strip mall. My money for his identity.

HUNGRY

Boss, that clinches it- the job is mine. I've got no problems
with temper or identity.

DON

True- but you are incredibly stupid. You are secretly a
member of PETA whose generous contributions shut down
the largest slaughterhouse in the United States.

HUNGRY

Yes, they're murderers. Cows have souls, tasty souls, but
souls nonetheless.

DON

A slaughterhouse unofficially owned by me. Quite a few of
my friends are out of their legitimate jobs because you're too
much of an idiot to know with whom you do business.
There you have it- you're all unworthy.

LUCKY

Boss, mine was an error of humanity, not stupidity.

HUNGRY

Mine was merely secondary.

RED

And mine was purely culinary.

LUCKY

Only you would joke at a time like this.

RED

Ah shut your yap.

LUCKY

Shut it for me.

HUNGRY

You said it, Marbury.

LUCKY

Go graze somewhere, herbivore. I bet you'll bleed
chlorophyll.

> (LUCKY, RED, *and* HUNGRY *draw their guns.*
> BUTCH *steps in front of the* DON *and raises his*
> *brick to strike.*)

BUTCH

Gun, gun!

DON

So, you're not as harmless as you otherwise might seem.
You've broken your trust with me again- but I have a
forgiving soul. You will hand over your guns this instant. If
anything happens to me, I have made arrangements that will
ruin you. Vanessa, why aren't you smiling?

VANESSA

Nothing about this is funny.

DON

Let's go for another smoke. I'll explain it to you. Butch, go
lock up their guns.

BUTCH

Will do, Boss.

> (BUTCH *exits with the guns.*)

End of Scene 1 option #1 (with food break):

DON
(To the audience and heads.) As for the rest of you. I've got eyes in this room whether I'm here or not. If you try something while I'm gone, I'm going to know, and it'll be the last thing you do. Now, because I'm so magnanimous, we have *[whatever dinner course is being served here]* ready for you. *[He explains how it will be served if necessary.]* Please enjoy it. I'll be back in a few minutes. Take your time. Vanessa.

*(*DON *exits with* VANESSA.*)*

END OF SCENE 1

End of Scene 1 option #2 (without food break):

DON
(To the audience and heads) As for the rest of you. I've got eyes in this room whether I'm here or not. If you try something while I'm gone, I'm going to know, and it'll be the last thing you do. Vanessa.

*(*DON *exits with* VANESSA.*)*

LUCKY
(To RED.*)* Why in the name of moonshine would you wave your piece around like that, huh?

RED
Don't you be blaming Samantha. 'Twas you and Hungry that drew first.

HUNGRY
Hey, I was just reacting.

RED

Is that right? How about I give ya something to react to right now?

HUNGRY

How are you gonna talk a big game without your big gun?

RED

I may not have Samantha, but I've got her five closest friends *(holds up her right hand and wiggles her fingers),* and they'll grip your throat as well as her handle.

> *(RED moves toward HUNGRY but LUCKY intervenes.)*

LUCKY

Y'all quit now! Didn't you hear the Don? He's watchin'. Probably got spies in each of our groups.

> *(The three heads slowly turn and look at their groups.)*

LUCKY

So let's just slow our roll, and play it cool. Got it?

HUNGRY

Yeah, okay.

RED

Aye, fine.

> *(Each head calmly returns to their group. HONEY slips into the kitchen area.)*

END OF SCENE 1

SCENE 2

(Each head interacts with their group. Perhaps they do some light interrogating about whether any audience members are spies for THE DON. BUTCH *returns from hiding the guns and patrols the room with his brick. Before the scene begins,* RED *and* HUNGRY *each find an excuse to leave the room.)*

LUCKY
(From across the room.) Butch! Come here.

*(*BUTCH *crosses to* LUCKY*)*

BUTCH
Okay. What?

LUCKY
So. Buddy. Wherever did you find to hide the guns? I'm sure you found some place really hard to find.

BUTCH
Yes. They're hidden.

LUCKY
Ain't you a kidder. I bet you would tell me if you checked your left pocket and found a thousand dollars in it.

*(*BUTCH *takes money out of his pocket.)*

BUTCH
I love it when I find money in my pocket!

LUCKY
So where are they hid?

BUTCH

You're funny.

(BUTCH leaves to continue to patrol the room.)

LUCKY

Yeah, you'll see how funny I can be.

(LUCKY starts to exit as RED enters from another door.)

RED

Where you going Lucky?

LUCKY

I gotta pee. Thanks for asking.

(He exits.)

RED

How you doin' there Butch?

BUTCH

Okay. How are you?

RED

I've been better. Ya see, I feel a bit naked.

BUTCH

You don't look naked.

RED

I'm using a metaphor, you dumb lout.

BUTCH

What's a meta for?

RED

I'm sayin' I feel like I'm missin' somethin' special.

BUTCH

Like love?

RED

No, my gun, you idiot! Without Samantha I get really irritable.

BUTCH

Who's Samantha?

RED

My gun! How would ya feel Butch, if someone took away your brick?

BUTCH

Nobody's gonna take Shelly away from me.

RED

But what I'm sayin'—Shelly?—what I'm sayin' is I feel like you would if I took your brick.

BUTCH

Boss, she's trying to take Shelly! BOSS!

RED

Butch! Shh..., calm down. I'm not trying to take your brick. I was just was wonderin' if you might help me get my baby back.

BUTCH

When did you have a baby?

RED

Butch, what's your favorite kind of brick?

BUTCH

Acme brand, Desert Mesa color.

RED

My brother works for Acme. You help me get my gun, and I can have a truckload of Acme Desert Mesa bricks delivered to your front door.

BUTCH

How soon?

RED

Within the week.

BUTCH

I'll have to ask the boss.

RED

No, no. No, you don't.

BUTCH

Then there's no deal.

> (BUTCH *walks away and* HONEY *comes to him.*)

HONEY

Butcheypoo?

BUTCH

No not yet, I haven't eaten.

HONEY

Focus dear. You know those itty-bitty guns you locked away not too long ago?

BUTCH

Yeah.

HONEY

Well, you know how afraid I am for you.

BUTCH

Yeah.

HONEY

And I know you want to be more than just a go-fer.

BUTCH

Honey, don't be silly, I'm not a gopher.

HONEY

Yes, you are. You just go for things.

BUTCH

I don't live in holes and tunnel systems.

HONEY

Focus, remember words have different meanings sometimes.

BUTCH

Yeah.

HONEY

Well, I know you don't want to be a mindless lackey all your life.

BUTCH

That's the truth. I'm tired of being ordered around.

HONEY

That's why I've got to see the guns. To check if they're loaded.

                              BUTCH

Okay.

                              HONEY

So come show me the guns.

                              BUTCH

No.

                    *(HONEY wraps her arms around him and kisses
                    him.)*

                              HONEY

How about now?

                              BUTCH

I don't think the boss would let me.

                              HONEY

Could we just for once forget the boss?

                              BUTCH

But then he'd cease to be the boss.

                              HONEY

Oh, never mind.

                    (HUNGRY *enters.)*

                              RED

Where were you?

                              HUNGRY

The kitchen. Got the chef to make me some tabouli.

                              RED

Was it good?

                            HUNGRY

I've had better—where you going?

                              RED

To find where the lout hid my gun.

                            HUNGRY

Oh, they're in the kitchen. Chef showed me, but they're
locked up pretty well.

                              RED

We'll see about that.

                    (She starts to exit to the kitchen.)

                            HUNGRY

Don't think you're gonna have any luck without Butch's
key.

                              RED

I just want to look at her.

                    (She exits into the kitchen. HUNGRY *sneaks up
                    behind* BUTCH *and taps him on the shoulder.
                    When* BUTCH *turns around,* HUNGRY *turns
                    with him so* BUTCH *doesn't see him.)*

                             BUTCH

Who did that?

                            HUNGRY

That was just me.

BUTCH

How did you do that? Did you disappear?

HUNGRY

No, I'm just sneaky. I used to be a magician.

BUTCH

Really?

HUNGRY

Nothing big. Just card tricks and stuff. Got a deck of cards?

BUTCH

No.

HUNGRY

Too bad, I could show you a great trick. Anyway, I presume Lucky and Red have each tried to get their guns from you.

BUTCH

Why would you think that?

HUNGRY

Don't give in to whatever they offer you. I don't care if it's money, power, whatever.

BUTCH

What about bricks?

HUNGRY

What?

BUTCH

Red offered me bricks. I like bricks.

HUNGRY

Even bricks. You don't know if they'll pull their gun on you.

(HONEY *comes over.*)

HONEY

Butchypoo, you're not going to let this man tell you what to do are you?

BUTCH

No.

HONEY

That's good. You've got to make your own decisions, haven't you?

BUTCH

Yes.

HONEY

That's right. Hungry, why don't you go eat something?

HUNGRY

Fine. I've got some tabouli in the back.

(He starts to leave.)

HONEY

Now wait a minute, I've got more I want to tell you. I'll be back, Butchypoo.

BUTCH

Okay.

(HONEY *goes to* HUNGRY.)

HONEY

Hungry, I'm sorry to be so mean. But I've got to keep up appearances with Butch.

HUNGRY

I get it. You just want to be closer to power, which apparently leaves me out. You forget that I hold a lot of power in New York, not to mention owning the biggest producer of vegan products outside of California, but that's apparently not enough.

HONEY

You have a chance here and now to take even more power.

HUNGRY

You heard the Don. He doesn't think I have what it takes.

HONEY

He doesn't have to think anything if you remove him from the picture.

HUNGRY

Are you suggesting—

HONEY

If you can find a way to take his place, I will ditch Butch and marry you. You can have me all to yourself.

HUNGRY

Honey, I'm not a criminal. Well, I am a criminal, but I'm not a murderer. What I mean to say is that while I'm a murderer in certain situations, this seems a little too much for me, especially while there's more tabouli in the kitchen.

(He exits to the kitchen as LUCKY *reenters.)*

                    HONEY

Lucky!

                    LUCKY

Yeah.

                    HONEY

I want to talk to you.

                    LUCKY

I thought we were keeping things between us quiet until all
this was done.

                    HONEY

I just wanted to tell you that Butch made me this great offer.

                    LUCKY

What do you mean?

                    HONEY

Did you know that he has loads of money from a rich
grandfather?

                    LUCKY

No.

                    HONEY

Apparently, he does, and he said that if I married him that I'd
never have to worry about money again.

                    LUCKY

If he's got all this money, then why's he working for the
Don?

                    HONEY

All I mean is that you have an opportunity to be number one,
more power, more money.

LUCKY

The Don ain't exactly happy with me, I'm sorry to say.

HONEY

He doesn't have to be if you make the decision for him in his...absence.

LUCKY

Are you suggesting that I kill the Don?

HONEY

I'm just thinking that you have an opportunity here you shouldn't pass up. I want to marry you, Lucky. But Butch is offering this to me, and it makes me think twice. You get the Don's place, and I won't even blink an eye—I'll be yours and only yours.

(He takes a drink from his flask.)

LUCKY

It could be a big mistake. Only I know you're worth it.

HONEY

That's right I am.

(They continue to talk quietly as RED *and* VANESSA *enter.)*

RED

You were here earlier. You know he has a problem with me temper.

VANESSA

I'm not suggesting that you simply step into his position. I'm suggesting that we work together. Your passion and my levelheadedness could get a lot done. And I know we both agree about the trouble with men in positions of leadership.

RED

Tell me about it.

VANESSA

I don't know how we'd do it. I'll leave you to figure things out. It was hard enough for me to get away from him to talk to you.

RED

I'll see what I can pull out of me noggin.

VANESSA

Good. I got to go check on him. I'll be back in a bit.

(She starts to exit as DON *re-enters.)*

DON

Butch, would you please make sure everyone is present.

BUTCH

Sure, boss, we just need Hungry.

*(*HUNGRY *enters with a granola bar.)*

BUTCH

There he is.

DON

Thank you, Butch.

HUNGRY

What?

DON

I am speaking to everyone now, thank you for your timely entrance.

HUNGRY

Don't mention it.

DON

First, I would like to acknowledge that I embarrassed all of you earlier. This is not an apology, rather it is to ensure you that I am completely aware of my actions, and my reasons for doing so are my own. Now, I will need to speak with each of you individually, without the ear and opinions of your fellow heads. This means that Butch will escort each of you Lucky, Red, and Hungry, back to the kitchen as a gathering area. I will send Vanessa to get the first of you in a minute. Butch, if you would, please.

BUTCH

Okay boss. Come with me or I'll hit you with my brick.

(Each head goes into the kitchen, followed by BUTCH. HONEY *remains in the room with* VANESSA *and* DON.)

DON

Honey, would you like to go with them?

HONEY and VANESSA

No thanks.

DON

Sorry, I was actually speaking to the woman named Honey, not you, honey.

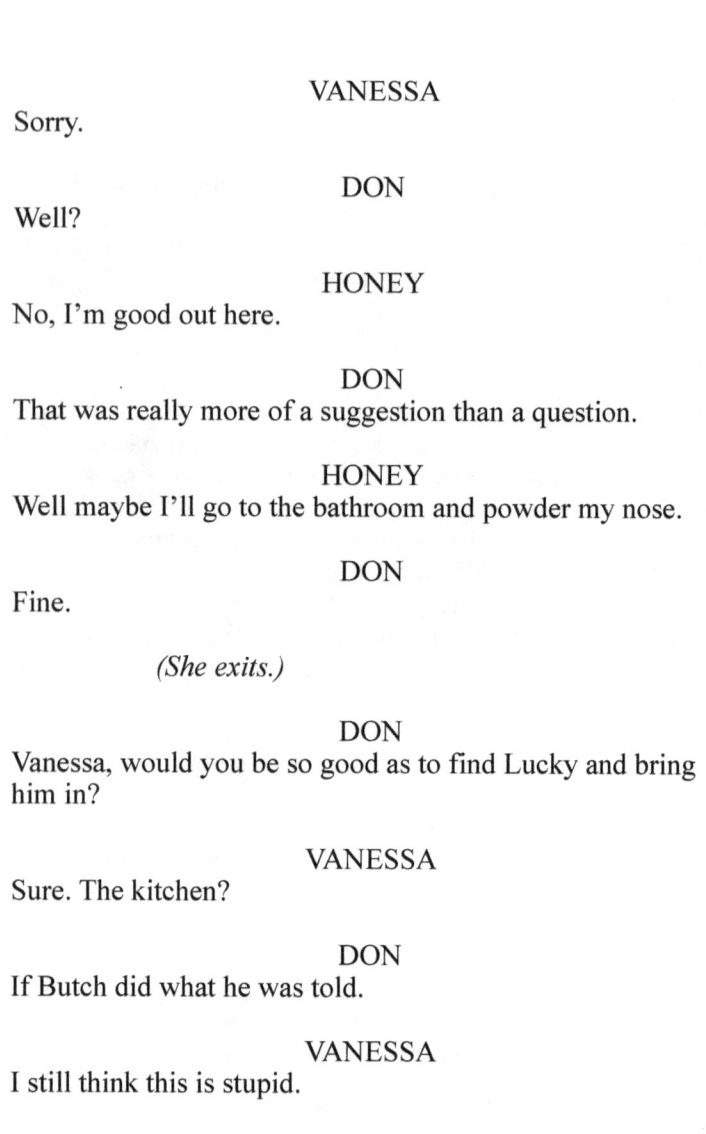

VANESSA

Sorry.

DON

Well?

HONEY

No, I'm good out here.

DON

That was really more of a suggestion than a question.

HONEY

Well maybe I'll go to the bathroom and powder my nose.

DON

Fine.

(She exits.)

DON

Vanessa, would you be so good as to find Lucky and bring him in?

VANESSA

Sure. The kitchen?

DON

If Butch did what he was told.

VANESSA

I still think this is stupid.

DON

Well, it's not your decision to make. Please bring in Lucky.

VANESSA

Sure. Honey.

(She exits.)

DON

(To the audience.) I trust each of you to pay attention, but not to get involved. I—

> *(A gunshot from the kitchen door. DON falls down dead. Silence. VANESSA runs in, the others follow soon after.)*

VANESSA

Don!

> *(She runs to him and checks his vitals.)*

VANESSA

He's dead. Who's got the gun? Everyone, show me your hands.

> *(Everyone does, nobody is holding a gun.)*

VANESSA

Well, someone had to have a gun- Butch, where are your keys?

BUTCH

Keys?

VANESSA

Yes, the ones you used to lock the guns up.

> *(BUTCH checks his pockets.)*

BUTCH

Yeah. They're not here.

VANESSA

[In this speech, references to locations can be changed to match the performance location.] Okay. Nobody call the police, we can deal with this ourselves. We do not need the police to find us all in here together. Butch, take the body into the kitchen. We need to search the area for an assassin. Honey, check the bathrooms. Butch, check the kitchen once you get the body in there. Lucky, head upstairs. Red, check outside. Hungry, check the lobby and stairway.

End of Scene 2 option #1 (with food break):

VANESSA

Meet back here in ten minutes.

> (*They exit to search as instructed.* BUTCH *starts to drag the body into the kitchen.*)

VANESSA

(*To the audience*) The rest of you, stay in this building. There's food, so it shouldn't be hard to stick around. *[Describe the food course and serving method as needed.]* I'm going to help the others search. Don't do anything rash. No police.

> (*She exits. Everyone follows suit as* BUTCH *drags the body into the kitchen.*)

END OF SCENE 2

End of Scene 2 option #2 (without food break):

VANESSA

Now!

(They exit to search as instructed. BUTCH *drags the body into the kitchen.)*

VANESSA

(To the audience.) The rest of you, I hope you were paying attention to everything, because we might need your help figuring this out. Do any of you have suspicions? Did you see anything you're willing to share? *[Hopefully a few audience members will share some observations. Thank each member after they share.]* Thanks, everyone, you've given me a lot to think about. Keep your eyes open until we get this thing figured out.

END OF SCENE 2

Scene 3

(If a break took place, LUCKY, RED, and HUNGRY may return and mingle with their people. If they do return, they will need to exit prior to the start of this scene. Enter BUTCH. If a break took place, enter VANESSA.)

VANESSA

Butch, did you check the guns?

BUTCH

Yeah.

VANESSA

How did you manage that? The keys were missing.

BUTCH

Oh, I found them in the lock.

VANESSA

Were any of them missing?

BUTCH

No, all the keys were there.

VANESSA

The guns, Butch, were any of them missing?

BUTCH

No, there were two of them.

VANESSA

Butch?

BUTCH

Yeah.

VANESSA

You hid three guns away.

BUTCH

Yes.

VANESSA

And you only saw two guns there?

BUTCH

That's right, two.

VANESSA

So, what would that indicate to you?

BUTCH

Five guns?

VANESSA

You're a complete waste, you know that right?

BUTCH

I do.

VANESSA

Whose gun was missing?

BUTCH

You mean the guns in the back? Oh, Red's was missing.

VANESSA

The one with the elephant ivory grips? Make sure you don't
tell Hungry, he's liable to blow his top.

(Enter HONEY, LUCKY, RED, and HUNGRY)

RED

Alright Vanessa, we want some answers.

HONEY

Where did you put our cars?

LUCKY

You don't trust us, and that's not right, lady.

HUNGRY

My pasta sauce had meat in it, and now I can't think of
anything but the imploring eyes of innocent calves who will
never know the comforting love of the udder that *you* stole
from them.

RED

Hungry. Focus now, me heart. Remember, we need to leave.

HUNGRY

Yeah, where's my car?

VANESSA

None of us are leaving until we find out who killed my husband. If you have a problem with that you will face the wrath of the brick- Butch.

BUTCH

Brick.

VANESSA

Here is what we will do. We are going to recreate every moment immediately before the murder. Even if we have to re-do everything we have done tonight, we will get this right and we will determine who did this.

RED

That might take hours.

VANESSA

Or longer if you don't cooperate. All of you assembled here, we need you to watch everything that just happened here and keep a sharp eye. You will help us understand who committed this crime. We are going to re-create this entire night.

(Enter MARLOWE.)

MARLOWE

Not so fast, Vanessa.

VANESSA

Don?

MARLOWE

I am not the Don.

LUCKY

You look just like him.

HUNGRY

The spitting image, except for the eye, of course.

HONEY

Hungry, your manners.

HUNGRY

Sorry, I didn't mean to mention your gimp.

RED

Cute.

MARLOWE

The Don...was my brother.

(DRAMATIC STINGER MUSIC CUE)

ALL

Ooooooh.

MARLOWE

That's right, "Oh." The kind of brother that makes you glad
your parents decided to have another go. Now which one of
you recidivists did him in?

ALL

Not me.

VANESSA

I never knew he had a brother.

MARLOWE

You have to protect your background toots; your husband knew that.

LUCKY

We never even knew his name.

MARLOWE

Because he kept it that way. My brother was a genius. He managed the double-life quite well.

RED

And what are you doing here?

HONEY

And how do you know your brother is dead?

HUNGRY

Some people believe that identical twins share a mystical bond that defies description. The National Identical Twin Center reports that some twins have sensed when the other is in danger, or even when they have died.

MARLOWE

He told me to be here for the meeting. I've been listening in.

HUNGRY

Oh.

LUCKY

So, what makes you think you can find the killer, Mr...?

MARLOWE

Call me Marlowe. And I used to be a cop. I'll find you out.

VANESSA

Exactly why did my husband ask you here?

MARLOWE

Don was going to retire tonight, and he had me bring some insurance for him. If any of you tried anything in his retirement, I was going to make some information known that would positively ruin you. I was going to come up and show you he meant business. But you wouldn't let him get that far, would you?

LUCKY

Hold it right there. How do you know it wasn't them? *(Indicates the audience.)* They were the only people in the room with the Don at the time.

MARLOWE

Nice try- but the audience doesn't count. Only one of you can be the killer, haven't you ever been to a murder mystery *[if you are not serving dinner, omit "dinner"]* dinner before?

VANESSA

So, what do you want to do, Mr. Marlowe?

MARLOWE

The only people who saw the murder are these people here. So, they are going to help figure out who did the crime. Now, I understand that each of you has a deputy here tonight. *(He speaks to the audience.)* If you're one of the deputies, raise your hand. *(Hopefully they do.)* Great. *(He gives each deputy a stack of sleuth sheets for their audience area.)* Hand these out to your people. With the help of my deputies here, each of you is gonna get a sleuth sheet – standard practice in the private eye business – and you're gonna fill them out for me; if you do it right, there may be a reward in it for you. And to give you a hand, I'm gonna tell you each of these people's secrets so you can judge whether or not they killed the Don.

RED

So, you're to be telling our secrets, will you now?

MARLOWE

That's right.

LUCKY

What makes you think you can tell these people those things and make it out alive, Marlowe?

MARLOWE

One simple reason- I am the detective.

HONEY

Sweetie, you mean *a* detective.

MARLOWE

No, I am *the* detective. I am the detective of this story. And the detective never dies. Oh, you can try but it won't work. Run me over, your car mysteriously pushes me into a ditch and I am perfectly fine, but for a bloody lip. Shoot me and it's always a shoulder wound with little-to-no blood. My brother chose well in me- he chose the immortal of the whodunit world.

VANESSA

He's right, you know.

MARLOWE

Anyone care to confess before we get down to it? I thought not.

> (MARLOWE *produces a large packet from underneath his coat. He tears into the packet which has several index cards.)*

RED

Marlowe, I think we can trust these good people to know who the killer is without hearing this nonsense.

MARLOWE

Alright, we'll start with you. (*Removes a red index card*) "Red" born Maureen Kathryn Sinead. First husband Bill O'Callaghan; second husband Stephen McGee.

RED

Go no farther, Marlowe I will have your other eye!

MARLOWE

Detective Marlowe, sunshine. Oh, this is great.

HUNGRY

Ooh tell us.

BUTCH

I love story time.

MARLOWE

It seems that the leader of the Boston Irish Crime Family is not Irish at all, and has only spoken with an Irish accent after watching "The Quiet Man."

LUCKY

Oh, your crew's going to love that.

MARLOWE

Hungry here, on the other hand—

HUNGRY

Mr. Marlowe. If you're anything like your brother, I presume you like a good smoke.

MARLOWE

It's one of my guilty pleasures.

HUNGRY

Might I offer you one of these fine Cuban cigars that I
happen to have in my jacket?

MARLOWE

Yes, you may.

(He takes it and puts it in his mouth unlit.)

MARLOWE

Thank you. Now, as I was saying, this New York City Crime
boss is a die-hard Boston Red Sox fan.

HUNGRY

Hey, I gave you a nice cigar. And no, it's not true. It's
not...alright I admit it. I am a sucker for losers. I watch every
game.

MARLOWE

Lucky's lucky flask? No liquor, but water. He's got
Hepatitis. Don't worry folks, the good kind.

HUNGRY

That's going too far! I should take my cigar back.

MARLOWE

You ain't getting nothing back.

VANESSA

Good. Now that we're done with that exercise, we can move
on to...

MARLOWE

Oh no, your husband had dirt on more than the bosses. You Vanessa, planned to usurp the power that the Don was giving up.

VANESSA

I have had enough! Butch, get rid of him.

MARLOWE

Butch has an IQ of 197.

LUCKY

You've got to have a misprint there.

MARLOWE

He's a world authority on the Thirty Years War and the Second Defenestration of Prague.

HONEY

What's a defestation?

BUTCH

Defenestration- it's when you throw someone out of a window. Yes, I fooled you all. I don't even like bricks. Thanks a lot, Marlowe- now all these people here know my secrets.

HONEY

So, what's my secret?

(She kisses him passionately.)

MARLOWE

You're having an affair with everyone in this room.

LUCKY

Um Marlowe, that's really no secret.

VANESSA

Yeah.

RED

He's right.

HUNGRY

Yep. We all knew that.

BUTCH

I sure did.

MARLOWE

Wait, there's more written here...Oh, and you keep a collection of toenail clippings from all of your lovers.

RED

Ew.

BUTCH

That's unique.

HUNGRY

Wait...how do you get them?

MARLOWE

So here we all are.

VANESSA

Yes, here we all are. And I am afraid that will be quite enough for you, Mr. Marlowe.

MARLOWE

So soon we forget, as detective I am immune to the machinations of the petty evil.

VANESSA

Butch, go get the guns.

BUTCH

Sure.

MARLOWE

This is unbelievable. You would think these people had never seen a mystery flick before. Let me tell you. Hungry gave me his cigar, right? Now knowing this criminal type, he's the Byzantine kind of guy who would keep a poisoned cigar on his person. But look. Here I chew it and I am perfectly fine. Honey.

HONEY

What?

MARLOWE

You kissed me passionately moments ago, right?

HONEY

Right.

MARLOWE

Now this is the femme fatale. And they always have some sort of poisoned something too. And it's often their lips.

(MARLOWE kisses HONEY again.)

MARLOWE

See, nothing. Now what did I tell you about being the Detective? Alright, here's the deal- fill out those sleuth sheets and one of us will be around to collect them. Give us your best guess as to who murdered the Don and why, and there will be a prize for the best one. It's warm in here, and this trench coat is unforgiving; can I get a drink?

VANESSA

Of course, I'll get it for you.

(She goes into the kitchen.)

RED

So why don't ya just figure out who did it yourself, huh?

MARLOWE

These here are witnesses, Red. Any good detective talks to witnesses.

(VANESSA comes back in with a glass of water.)

VANESSA

Here you go.

MARLOWE

Thank you. *(He takes a sip.)* Now, as I was saying...man it's hot in here.

VANESSA

Something the matter, detective?

MARLOWE

Wouldn't you like that? I just need to---

(MARLOWE falls down, dead. Enter BUTCH.)

BUTCH

That sucks. Alright people. Get working on those sheets, folks.

End of Scene 3 option #1 (with food break):

VANESSA

That's right. And nobody leaves! Lucky, Red, Hungry, Honey – you stick around and answer any questions these people have. And people – when you're done with your sheets, you give them to your deputy. Deputies, once you have them all, give your stack to me or Butch. There's more food, so you're going to have to multitask. *[Describe the food course and how it will be served as necessary.]* Last call for those sheets is ten minutes, so get to asking questions and filling them out. Don't let the good food distract you. Oh Butch?

BUTCH

Yes Vanessa.

VANESSA

Are they supposed to solve the murder of the Don or the Detective, or both, or what?

BUTCH

(BUTCH *looks at a spare sleuth sheet.)* The Don. Just the Don. No one cares about detectives, even if they are twins of the Don.

RED

Are we sure they're not triplets?

BUTCH

Oh, don't be absurd. Who keeps an identical sibling secret anyway?

> (BUTCH *drags off* MARLOWE *and then re-enters to help* VANESSA *gather the sheets. They mill about until everyone has handed in a sheet and then take the sheets off stage for the* MARLOWE *actor look them over.* LUCKY, RED, HUNGRY, *and* HONEY *answer any*

questions the audience members may have for
them.)

END OF SCENE 3

End of Scene 3 option #2 (without food break):

VANESSA

That's right. And nobody leaves! Lucky, Red, Hungry,
Honey – you stick around and answer any questions these
people have. And people – when you're done with your
sheets, you give them to your deputy. Deputies, once you
have them all, give your stack to me or Butch. I'll give you
five minutes to ask any questions and get your sheets filled
out, so get to work. Oh Butch?

BUTCH

Yes Vanessa.

VANESSA

Are they supposed to solve the murder of the Don or the
Detective, or both, or what?

BUTCH

(BUTCH *looks at a spare sleuth sheet.)* The Don. Just the
Don. No one cares about detectives, even if they are twins
of the Don.

RED

Are we sure they're not triplets?

BUTCH

Oh, don't be absurd. Who keeps an identical sibling secret
anyway?

(BUTCH *drags off* MARLOWE *and then re-*
enters to help VANESSA *answer questions and*

*gather the sheets from the deputies. They mill
about until everyone has handed in a sheet and
then take the sheets off stage for the
MARLOWE actor to look them over. LUCKY,
RED, HUNGRY, and HONEY chat with the
audience for as long as it takes to get sleuth
sheets taken care of.)*

END OF SCENE 3

Scene 4: option 1 (Hungry is the killer)

(Enter VANESSA and BUTCH.)

VANESSA
Lucky! Red! Hungry! Honey! Get over here. Line up. We're
going to find out who killed the Don.

(They line up at the front of the room.)

VANESSA
Butch, tell each of them what these good people revealed to
us with their writings.

BUTCH
Honey: you tried to convince Hungry and Lucky to kill the
Don for you. That means that they each had a motive – you.
That also means that if it was one of them, you are
incriminated as well. Lucky: you tried to bribe me into
giving you your gun back. The bribe? Money. Little did you
know that I have all of the money I need through the sales of
my best-selling non-fiction book on the second
defenestration of Prague. Red: you amateur, you tried to
bribe me with bricks. How dumb do you think I am?

HUNGRY

I never tried to bribe you.

BUTCH

No, you didn't. But you did take my key, you former magician. When you were giving me that pep-talk about not letting people bribe me, you pulled a slight of hand trick and got my keys.

HUNGRY

Why would I do a thing like that? Come on, Butch, we're pals, don't you trust me?

BUTCH

Not a whit.

HUNGRY

Fine.

(He pulls out a gun.)

RED

Samantha! You vicious brute, how could you Bogart an honest woman's "boom-stick"?

HUNGRY

That's right Red, I stole Samantha and used her to kill the Don. You couldn't leave well enough alone, could you? You all just had to know who did the crime, who done it? Well, I did and I am glad.

But you people don't realize I was going to use my power for good. Don't you realize that every day we destroy innocent lives? Lives that could have easily been saved if we just sat up and listened. Yes, I would have used my power to save the North American Bison.

Consider- was one corrupt murderer's life of any more worth than the beautiful elegant buffalo I could have saved? You,

the carnivorous elite would have given your power to
another greedy criminal.
Not now. I have the gun, so I have the power and you will
obey me!

RED

You know the grips on that gun are made of elephant's tusks,
right?

> (HUNGRY *yelps pathetically and drops the gun.*
> VANESSA *sneaks up behind him and grabs*
> *him.* BUTCH *then takes the gun off the ground*
> *and turns it on* HUNGRY.)

BUTCH

Thank you, Vanessa, good thinking Red.

VANESSA

You're welcome, sweetie.

HONEY

Sweetie? That's my man.

VANESSA

Honey, he's been my man for years. You thought the Don
was the only one with a little extra-marital excitement?
Butch, take him out to a nice, quiet location. We don't want
to spoil dinner for these nice people. Make sure the
authorities never find him.

BUTCH

Sure thing schnookems.

HUNGRY

Wait! You can't do this, I'm a crime boss! And besides, someone else killed the detective. I never poison my cigars. Someone else here is guilty, and I know who!

HONEY

Hungry, don't tell him it was me!

BUTCH

Honey?

HONEY

I shouldn't have said that.

RED

You're right, you shouldn't have.

HONEY

But didn't we all want him out of here? He would've ratted us all out! Besides, he was a detective, it wasn't like he was a real person. Butch you never liked him anyway.

VANESSA

And I don't like you going after my man. Butch, take her with you, somewhere quiet.

BUTCH

Come on, Honey.

HONEY

Oh Butch, can't we put this behind us? Can't we just kiss and make up?

BUTCH

You aren't kissing anyone anymore.

(BUTCH exits with HUNGRY in one hand and HONEY in the other.)

VANESSA

Red, Lucky, your cars are over at *[nearby location]*. Your guns will be delivered to you within the week. Butch is the new Don, and you will treat him with more respect than you treated my most recent husband.

RED

Sure thing.

LUCKY

Yes ma'am.

VANESSA

Get out of here.

(They exit.)

VANESSA

(To the audience.) And the rest of you – you keep quiet about this evening, or there will be consequences. Drive safe now.

(She exits.)

END OF SCENE 4 (see Curtain Call)

Scene 4: option 2 (Lucky is the killer)

(Enter VANESSA and BUTCH.)

VANESSA

Lucky! Red! Hungry! Honey! Get over here. Line up. We're going to find out who killed the Don.

(They line up at the front of the room.)

VANESSA

Butch, tell each of them what these good people revealed to us with their writings.

BUTCH

Honey: you tried to convince Hungry and Lucky to kill the Don for you. That means that they each had a motive – you. That also means that if it was one of them, you are incriminated as well. Red: you tried to bribe me into giving you your gun back. The bribe? Bricks. How dumb do you think I am? Don't answer, it's a rhetorical question. Lucky, you tried to bribe me too. With money. Little did you know that I have all of the money I need through the sales of my best-selling non-fiction book on the second defenestration of Prague.

LUCKY

Honest mistake.

BUTCH

Yeah, but not an honest bribe. While you were slipping money into my pocket, you were also taking my keys.

LUCKY

I ain't no pickpocket.

BUTCH

Then empty your pockets.

LUCKY

Fine.

(He pulls out a gun.)

RED

Samantha! You vicious brute, how could you Bogart an honest woman's "boom-stick"?

LUCKY

That's right Red, I stole your bullet spitter and used it to kill the Don. You couldn't let sleeping dogs lie, could you? You all just had to know who kilt him. Well, I did. There, happy now?

HUNGRY

Why, Lucky?

LUCKY

Oh, come on, all y'all were thinkin about it. I'm just the one who had the skivvies to do it. I was gettin tired of the whole pretend redneck life. I want out of Kentucky; I want to be metropolitan.

HUNGRY

You can drop the accent, then.

LUCKY

I can't, it's too ingrained! That's why I have to get out. And because I have the gun, none of y'all are gonna stop me from taking control!

(BUTCH, who has been sneaking up behind LUCKY, swiftly and simply takes the gun out of LUCKY's hand.)

BUTCH

That was easy. I didn't even have to use my brick.

(VANESSA grabs LUCKY from behind.)

LUCKY

Dagnabbit.

BUTCH

Thank you, Vanessa.

VANESSA

You're welcome, sweetie.

HONEY

Sweetie? That's my man.

VANESSA

Honey, he's been my man for years. You thought the Don was the only one with a little extra-marital excitement? Butch, take him out to a nice, quiet location. We don't want to spoil dinner for these nice people. Make sure the authorities never find him.

BUTCH

Sure thing schnookems.

LUCKY

Wait! You can't do this, I'm a crime boss! And besides, someone else killed the detective, and I know who!

HONEY

Lucky, don't tell him it was me!

BUTCH

Honey?

HONEY

I shouldn't have said that.

RED

You're right, you shouldn't have.

HONEY

But didn't we all want him out of here? He would've ratted
us all out! Besides, he was a detective, it wasn't like he was
a real person. Butch, you never liked him anyway.

VANESSA

And I don't like you going after my man. Butch, take her
with you, somewhere quiet.

BUTCH

Come on, Honey.

HONEY

Oh Butch, can't we put this behind us? Can't we just kiss
and make up?

BUTCH

You aren't kissing anyone anymore.

> (BUTCH *exits with* LUCKY *in one hand and*
> HONEY *in the other.)*

VANESSA

Red, Hungry, your cars are over at [nearby location]. Your
guns will be delivered to you within the week. Butch is the
new Don, and you will treat him with more respect than you
treated my most recent husband.

RED

Sure thing.

LUCKY

Yes ma'am.

VANESSA

Get out of here.

(They exit.)

VANESSA

(To the audience.) And the rest of you – you keep quiet about this evening, or there will be consequences. Drive safe now.

(She exits.)

END OF SCENE 4 (see Curtain Call)

Scene 4: option 3 (Honey is the killer)

(Enter VANESSA and BUTCH.)

VANESSA

Lucky! Red! Hungry! Honey! Get over here. Line up. We're going to find out who killed the Don.

(They line up at the front of the room.)

VANESSA

Butch, tell each of them what these good people revealed to us with their writings.

BUTCH

Honey: you tried to convince Hungry and Lucky to kill the Don for you. That means that they each had a motive – you. That also shows that you wanted him dead. Lucky: you tried to bribe me into giving you your gun back. The bribe? Money. Little did you know that I have all of the money I need through the sales of my best-selling non-fiction book on the second defenestration of Prague. Red: you amateur, you tried to bribe me with bricks. How dumb do you think I am?

HUNGRY

I never tried to bribe you.

BUTCH

No, you didn't. But you did have an opportunity to take my keys, you former magician. When you were giving me that pep-talk about not letting people bribe me, you might have pulled a slight of hand trick and got my keys.

HUNGRY

But I didn't.

BUTCH

Or Lucky. You could have taken my keys when you slipped bribery money into my pocket.

LUCKY

Shucks, you're right. That would'a been a good idea.

BUTCH

Sometimes we just let opportunities pass us by, like strangers on a busy sidewalk, never truly knowing the possibilities that might have been.

LUCKY

Right.

BUTCH

But it was Honey who distracted me the most.

HONEY

Me?

BUTCH

When you put your lips on mine, the rest of the world fell away for an instant, leaving me vulnerable to your thieving hands.

*(HONEY pulls out the gun and points it at
BUTCH)*

HONEY

Sorry, sweetie. But a girl's gotta do what a girl's gotta do.

RED

Samantha! You double-crossing vixen, how could you
Bogart an honest woman's "boom-stick"?

HONEY

That's right Red, I stole Samantha and used it to kill the
Don. It became clear none of you were going to do it for
me, so I had to take matters into my own hands. But now
that I've taken care of the Don, one of you needs to rise to
the occasion. Lucky, Red, and Hungry—one of you needs to
take his place, and I'll be there by your side. Convince me
you should be the one, and help me kill the others.

> *(During HONEY's speech, VANESSA has been
> sneaking around behind HONEY and once the
> speech is done, manages to knock HONEY out—
> maybe a head-butt, maybe she was able to pick
> something up to knock her out with. Regardless,
> HONEY falls to the ground.)*

BUTCH

Thank you Vanessa.

VANESSA

You're welcome, sweetie.

RED

Sweetie?

VANESSA

What, you thought the Don was the only one with a little
extra-marital excitement? Butch, take her out to a nice, quiet
location. We don't want to spoil dinner for these nice
people. Make sure the authorities never find her.

BUTCH

Sure thing schnookems.

LUCKY

Ain't we forgetting something? Who killed the detective? Or
did she do that, too?

HUNGRY

Oh, no, that was me. But I was pretty sure we all wanted him
taken out, right? He had dirt on all of us.

> *(Everyone responds in general agreement.
> VANESSA picks up the gun.)*

VANESSA

Red, Lucky, your cars are over at *[nearby location]*. Your
guns will be delivered to you within the week.

RED

Can I just take Samantha now?

VANESSA

No. From now on, Butch is the new Don, and you will treat
him with more respect than you treated my most recent
husband.

RED

Sure thing.

LUCKY

Yes ma'am.

VANESSA

Get out of here.

(They exit.)

VANESSA

(To the audience.) And the rest of you – you keep quiet about this evening, or there will be consequences. Drive safe now.

(She exits.)

END OF SCENE 4 (see Curtain Call)

Scene 4: option 4 (Butch is the killer)

(Enter VANESSA and BUTCH.)

VANESSA

Lucky! Red! Hungry! Honey! Get over here. Line up. We're going to find out who killed the Don.

(They line up at the front of the room.)

VANESSA

Butch, tell each of them what these good people revealed to us with their writings.

BUTCH

Honey: you tried to convince Hungry and Lucky to kill the Don for you. That means that they each had a motive – you. That also means that if it was one of them, you are incriminated as well. Lucky: you tried to bribe me into giving you your gun back. The bribe? Money. Little did you know that I have all of the money I need through the sales of my best-selling non-fiction book on the second

BUTCH (CONT)

defenestration of Prague. Red: you amateur, you tried to
bribe me with bricks. How dumb do you think I am?

HUNGRY

I never tried to bribe you.

BUTCH

No, you didn't. But you did take my key, you former
magician. When you were giving me that pep-talk about not
letting people bribe me, you pulled a slight of hand trick and
got my keys.

HUNGRY

Why would I do a thing like that? Okay, I did try, but your
keys weren't in your pocket. In fact, they weren't anywhere
on your person. You must have used them.

BUTCH

Come on now, who's going to believe this?

HUNGRY

Fine, turn out your pockets.

VANESSA

Do it, Butch.

LUCKY

Real slow.

(Butch pulls out a gun.)

RED

Samantha! You vicious brute, how could you Bogart an
honest woman's "boom-stick"?

BUTCH

That's right, Red, I stole Samantha and used it to kill the
Don. You couldn't leave well enough alone, could you? You
all just had to know who did the crime, who done it? Well, I
did and I am glad.
The Don never appreciated I was smarter than him. He
searched for every tiny chance to put me down. Then my
book came out and he found a split infinitive! He wouldn't
let it go. He'd look up examples of split infinitives just to
viciously mock me with them! He wouldn't shut up about it.
Well, I shut him up!

> (*During* BUTCH's *monologue,* LUCKY *sneaks
> up behind him and grabs the gun.* LUCKY *holds
> the gun on* BUTCH.)

VANESSA

Good moves, Lucky. Keep the gun on him. I can't believe I
carried on with you, schnookems.

HONEY

Schnookems? That's my man.

VANESSA

Honey, he's been my man for years. You thought the Don
was the only one with a little extra-marital excitement? But
that won't save him now. Take him out to a nice, quiet
location. We don't want to spoil dinner for these nice people.
Make sure the authorities never find him.

LUCKY

Sure thing.

VANESSA

One more thing, Butch. You said "...to viciously mock." Isn't
that a split infinitive?

BUTCH

No! He's got me saying them, too! Wait! Someone else killed the detective, it wasn't me! Someone else here is guilty, and I know who!

HONEY

Butch, don't tell him it was me!

HUNGRY

Honey?

HONEY

I shouldn't have said that.

RED

You're right, you shouldn't have.

HONEY

But didn't we all want him out of here? He would've ratted us all out! Besides, he was a detective, it wasn't like he was a real person. Butch you never liked him anyway.

VANESSA

And I didn't like you going after my man, but now you get to go with him.

HUNGRY

Come on, Honey.

HONEY

Oh Hungry, can't we put this behind us? Can't we just kiss and make up?

HUNGRY

You aren't kissing anyone anymore.

(HUNGRY exits with BUTCH in one hand and HONEY in the other.)

VANESSA

Red, Lucky, your cars are over at *[nearby location]*. Your guns will be delivered to you within the week. I am the new Don, and you will treat me with more respect than you treated my most recent husband.

RED

Sure thing.

LUCKY

Yes ma'am.

VANESSA

Get out of here.

(They exit.)

VANESSA

(To the audience.) And the rest of you – you keep quiet about this evening, or there will be consequences. Drive safe now.

(She exits.)

END OF SCENE 4 (see Curtain Call)

Scene 4: option 5 (Red is the killer)

(Enter VANESSA and BUTCH.)

VANESSA

Lucky! Red! Hungry! Honey! Get over here. Line up. We're going to find out who killed the Don.

(They line up at the front of the room.)

VANESSA

Butch, tell each of them what these good people revealed to us with their writings.

BUTCH

Honey: you tried to convince Hungry and Lucky to kill the Don for you. That means that they each had a motive – you. That also means that if it was one of them, you are incriminated as well. Lucky: you tried to bribe me into giving you your gun back. The bribe? Money. Little did you know that I have all of the money I need through the sales of my best-selling non-fiction book on the second defenestration of Prague. Red: you amateur, you tried to bribe me with bricks. How dumb do you think I am?

HUNGRY

I never tried to bribe you.

BUTCH

No, you didn't. But you did take my key, you former magician. When you were giving me that pep-talk about not letting people bribe me, you pulled a slight of hand trick and got my keys.

HUNGRY

Yes, I did! But by the time I got near the kitchen I'd lost the key.

RED

A likely story! Well, I am relieved! Come now, let's take the law into our own hands, no need to investigate further. Quickly now; he must be the one.

BUTCH

Must he, Red? You're pretty fast to punish him. Why did he
go for your gun? You carry a hand cannon. Could Hungry lift
the thing? No. Whoever took your Samantha knew how to
use it. Maybe we should search you.

RED

That's close enough!

(She pulls out Samantha.)

RED

I freed my sweet Samantha and used it to kill the Don. You
couldn't leave well enough alone, could you? You all just
had to know who did the crime, who done it? Well, I did and
I am glad.
Do you know what that man did? We in the great city of
Boston have been celebrating St. Patricks' Day since 1737!
We're the first and finest.
That Don had the unparalleled gall to tell me that Boston's
St. Patrick's Day parade didn't hold a candle to the one in
New York City! Imagine, New York City! He said we
weren't even as good as Chicago!
Now, Normally I'm liberal-minded, but I'm wildly
belligerent about my beloved Boston, so I sent the Don to
meet his maker. And you are all gonna be next! "SWEET
CAROLINE!"

(VANESSA *sneaks up behind* RED *and grabs
her.* BUTCH *then takes the gun and turns it on*
RED)

BUTCH

Thank you, Vanessa, good thinking.

VANESSA

You're welcome, sweetie.

HONEY

Sweetie? That's my man.

VANESSA

Honey, he's been my man for years. You thought the Don was the only one with a little extra-marital excitement? Butch, take her out to a nice, quiet location. We don't want to spoil dinner for these nice people. Make sure the authorities never find her.

BUTCH

Sure thing schnookems.

RED

Wait! You got me fair and square, but I didn't whack the detective. Someone else here is guilty, and I know who!

HONEY

Red, don't tell him it was me!

BUTCH

Honey?

HONEY

I shouldn't have said that.

LUCKY

You're right, you shouldn't have.

HONEY

But didn't we all want him out of here? He would've ratted us all out! Besides, he was a detective, it wasn't like he was a real person. Butch you never liked him anyway.

VANESSA

And I don't like you going after my man. Butch, take her
with you, somewhere quiet.

BUTCH

Come on, Honey.

HONEY

Oh Butch, can't we put this behind us? Can't we just kiss
and make up?

BUTCH

You aren't kissing anyone anymore.

> (BUTCH *exits with* RED *in one hand and*
> HONEY *in the other.)*

VANESSA

Hungry, Lucky, your cars are over at *[nearby location]*.
Your guns will be delivered to you within the week. Butch is
the new Don, and you will treat him with more respect than
you treated my most recent husband.

RED

Sure thing.

LUCKY

Yes ma'am.

VANESSA

Get out of here.

> *(They exit.)*

VANESSA

(To the audience.) And the rest of you – you keep quiet about
this evening, or there will be consequences. Drive safe now.

(She exits.)

END OF SCENE 4 (see Curtain Call)

Scene 4: option 6 (Vanessa is the killer)

(Enter VANESSA and BUTCH.)

VANESSA

Lucky! Red! Hungry! Honey! Get over here. Line up. We're going to find out who killed the Don.

(They line up at the front of the room.)

VANESSA

Butch, tell each of them what these good people revealed to us with their writings.

BUTCH

Honey: you tried to convince Hungry and Lucky to kill the Don for you. That means that they each had a motive – you. That also means that if it was one of them, you are incriminated as well. Lucky: you tried to bribe me into giving you your gun back. The bribe? Money. Little did you know that I have all of the money I need through the sales of my best-selling non-fiction book on the second defenestration of Prague. Red: you amateur, you tried to bribe me with bricks. How dumb do you think I am?

HUNGRY

I never tried to bribe you.

BUTCH

No, you didn't. But you did take my key, you former magician. When you were giving me that pep-talk about not letting people bribe me, you pulled a slight of hand trick and got my keys.

HUNGRY

Okay, that's true, but I didn't kill the Don. I just felt unsafe without my gun.

BUTCH

So, you admit to having your gun?

HUNGRY

I was unlocking the safe when I heard the gunshot go off, and I grabbed the first gun I saw. Here.

(He pulls out a gun.)

RED

Samantha! You vicious brute, how could you Bogart an honest woman's "boom-stick"?

HUNGRY

I was scared!

BUTCH

I don't believe you, but we should search everyone else before we jump to conclusions. Vanessa, search Red and Honey.

RED

Wait a fine minute, me lad, you and Vanessa should be searched, too.

BUTCH

Fine. Vanessa, you first.

(As BUTCH *steps toward* VANESSA*, she pulls out a gun and points it at him.)*

VANESSA

Don't bother. You might like us to believe you aren't stupid, Butch, but you weren't smart enough to check me for a gun before, were you?

HONEY

Hold on, it was you?

VANESSA

No, it was Butch.

HONEY

Butch, I'm shocked.

VANESSA

Of *course* it was me, homewrecker. You think the Don was easy to live with? You think someone with my talent could stand around and play the wife forever? No. Especially not to a man who chose to give up his power. I deserve to stand on top of the mountain of crime, and tonight was my chance. And without your guns, none of you can stop me!

*(*BUTCH *points the gun he holds at* VANESSA*.)*

BUTCH

Samantha can.

(The two have a brief standoff. During BUTCH's *next line,* LUCKY *sneaks up behind* VANESSA*.)*

BUTCH

What if we share it? The top of the mountain. You can even
have it in name.

> (LUCKY *takes the gun from* VANESSA *and
> pushes her to* BUTCH.)

BUTCH

Too late. Thanks, Lucky.

VANESSA

Now wait, let's talk about this.

BUTCH

There is nothing to talk about. I'll decide who gets to be the
Don. Lucky and Red, take her out a nice, quiet location.

LUCKY

You got it.

> *(They start to drag her off.)*

VANESSA

Wait, you can't do this. Besides, I didn't kill the detective.
Someone else did that, and I know who.

HONEY

Vanessa, don't tell him it was me!

BUTCH

Honey?

HONEY

I shouldn't have said that.

RED

You're right, you shouldn't have.

HONEY

But didn't we all want him out of here? He would've ratted us all out! Besides, he was a detective, it wasn't like he was a real person. Butch you never liked him anyway.

BUTCH

And I don't like us killing people we don't have to. We're criminals, not animals. Hungry, take her the same place they take Vanessa.

HUNGRY

Come on, Honey.

HONEY

Oh Hungry, can't we put this behind us? Can't we just kiss and make up?

HUNGRY

You aren't kissing anyone anymore.

(Everyone but BUTCH exits.)

BUTCH *(to the audience)*

I trust the rest of you keep quiet about this evening, or there will be consequences. Drive safe now.

(She exits.)

END OF SCENE 4 (see Curtain Call)

Curtain Call

(The actors return to the room to take a bow. The final actor is the one who played

MARLOWE. What follows is optional, but recommended.)

MARLOWE ACTOR
(Addresses the audience. The speech may be improvised, written out in advance, or a mix of both. The bullet points below are the recommended elements of the speech. You may also use or adapt the sample below for your specific staging.)

- Thank the audience for their attendance and participation, along with a special thank you to the deputies.
- If there are cooks and servers, thank them and perhaps encourage a round of applause for them.
- Congratulate the audience for their excellent sleuthing.
- Announce an audience member who guessed the killer correctly. This may be drawn from a hat containing all of the correct guesses, or it is one selected for having the best explanation.
- Award the audience member a prize. This can be anything from free tickets to the next production, to theatre swag, to a brick signed by Butch.
- Swear the audience to secrecy and wish them a good night.

Sample Curtain Speech

MARLOWE ACTOR
Everyone, thank you for coming out to see the show. And a special thanks for those who were our deputies and everyone who helped decide who our killer is. *[If you are doing this as a dinner show, include-]* Let's give a big round of applause to everyone who prepared and served this delicious meal! *[If you aren't doing a dinner show, proceed to-]* Now comes the part when we honor the excellent sleuth of the night, the

MARLOWE ACTOR (CONT)

person who not only fingered the killer, but gave the best explanation for why *[insert name of character who killed the Don]* killed the Don. Our super sleuth is *[name of the person]*, and their reason for the murder was *[reason they stated]*. *[Optional if you have gifts]* We have some gifts for our super sleuth this- *[free tickets, swag, a signed brick, whatever you choose to make a gift.]* Finally, we have something to ask of you. In a grand old theater tradition, we are going to swear you to silence regarding the killer and the solution. Please raise your right hands and repeat after me- "I, your name *[some people will say "your name," react appropriately]* do solemnly swear that I will not reveal the solemn secrets of Mountain of Crime, or may I be beaten silly with Butch's brick." Thank you all again, and have safe travels home.

(All actors exit.)

END OF PLAY